Pitch To Me Online

A Ca$h Course in Today's Film Finance

First Edition

Harold Lewis

In The Lab Publishing

Los Angeles California

DEDICATION

This book is dedicated to my superhero mother, Bobbie Ruth Lewis, who encouraged me to take risks and to not fear spiders.

When I was about eight years old, my mother had my four siblings and me working out in the front yard pulling weeds. Suddenly, I looked up and saw a big black widow spider in my face. Naturally I screamed because, as you all know for a fact, the prevailing conventional wisdom among eight year-olds is that black widows are the most dangerous predators in the yard and they are always trying to kill you!

Anyway, instead of my mother coming to my rescue and consoling me, she reached her hand out into its web and squished that spider between her bare fingers! She then said to me "this little thing is not going to hurt you, but if you don't finish pulling those weeds I will!". Needless to say, I was traumatized, but at the same time I was so excited about the story I was going to tell my friends about my invincible mom the next day at school!

My mom instantly became my hero! Being an only parent with five kids, my mother's lessons by necessity were always immediate, significant, and memorable!

I gained so much valuable insight from her not just that day, but throughout my life. She not only helped me overcome any fear, but she also taught me that sometimes by taking risks you are made stronger!

This book is in part about understanding risk to minimize fear and how you use these tools to strengthen your outcomes in film finance.

ACKNOWLEDGEMENTS

I want to first thank my business partner and mentor Brenda Flewellyn. Brenda is a true pioneer and has provided me with so much insight in the world of film finance! Thanks to my good friend Varshini Soobiah for her words of wisdom. I also want to thank my friend and fellow author Michael Perrotta for all his continued encouragement and sharing. To my muse Natasha Stevens, thank you so much for letting me have access to your incredible memory! Thanks to my best friend Al Jones for always being there! To my big brother Preston Lewis I say you are simply amazing and the best person I have ever known! Finally, I want to thank all of you eager filmmakers that inspired me to create www. pitch2me.net so that we together can make the process of independent film finance more efficient.

TABLE OF CONTENTS

PREFACE

I have spent hundreds of hours intently listening to filmmakers pitch their projects to my partner, our staff, and me. Some of the ideas were great and some were not so great, but one thing's for sure: **_ALL_** of the filmmakers were intensely passionate about their projects!

Getting someone to listen to your pitch brings hope, but it's truly a numbers game. You have to hustle around and talk to as many people as will listen. Most of the time you have to trek out to Los Angeles or New York or Atlanta and try to make as many appointments as you can. Sometimes you can be a little more efficient by attending AFM, Cannes or other Film Festivals. You can even go to film finance seminars and try to make connections with film financiers.

Sometimes these methods work but often it only serves as practice for your pitch (and practice is good). You never know until afterwards if you are getting to the right person (defined as: one who can write a check). This can be a very laborious task for most of us but it's how deals have gotten done for years. Is there a better, more efficient way?

For years, my partner and I have struggled to find the answer to this question; one that would allow filmmakers an opportunity to efficiently reach as many potential financiers as possible.

Another goal of ours was to provide a way for those who don't make scriptwriting a profession but may have written a Screenplay, or TV Show, or Documentary and would like to test its viability in the open market; an opportunity for dreams that might otherwise be left to mold in a desk drawer, or forgotten in a computer file, or lost in the recesses of ones mind to get a chance to be fulfilled.

I have also had too many conversations with people who constantly complain about content on TV or at the theater which they deem, for their own reasons, to be subpar, garbage, or too stereotypical. These people also claim that they would like to change the images that they see and are willing to put their money where their mouth is if given the opportunity. How can this be done?

I have been all over the globe looking for money to fund our client's projects and one thing that I have learned is that, as opportunistic as money is, it rarely comes looking for you! And there is a reason this is the case: sometimes money does not know the best places to go — just like ideas don't know the best place to go for money.

And this question (the best place to go) led to the conclusion that online professional funding is the way of the future of independent film finance.

United States Supreme Court Justice William Brennan coined the term "The Marketplace Of Ideas". Now, I'm sure he was not referring exclusively to the film business; nevertheless he was spot-on! We need a place to efficiently allow ideas and capital to meet. I believe that a well-constructed, private, online marketspace serves this purpose. The rationale for this platform is simple: it saves time, money, and offers the widest professional audience. We know it works well for Crowd Funding and it also works for Professional Funding.

This book is not intended to be an exhaustive textbook as to how to finance a film; that would take many volumes. It also makes no claims to be substitute for research and due diligence; legal, financial or otherwise. There are many resources available to educate one on the details of this highly intricate process.

Our desire is to open the opportunity for filmmakers to procure funding and to expand the field of potential financiers. Ultimately we would like to achieve a situation where there would be a constant and predictable flow of capital to finance worthy film projects without the need to jump from one financing scheme to another.

Some may argue that this is a bold and ambitious goal. And we concur with that assessment. However, we believe the time is right and the time is now! There is an every increasing capacity for content and we believe this condition creates opportunity for financing like never before!

To those of you that are highly experienced in the realm of film finance or have open access to unlimited amount of funds or can walk in to any studio and demand a meeting with a top exec, this may not be the book for you. Those of us mere and humble mortals on the other hand can use all the resources we can get and this book is designed for us!

So, unless your name is Spielberg, Howard, Gruber, Abrams, Bay, or Perry, please read on and you might just get rewarded with a gem or two to help you succeed!!

Pitch What?

Real Estate: LOCATION! LOCATION! LOCATION!

Film: STORY! STORY! STORY!

If you listen to film critics (especially those who have never written a successful script), they often complain and denigrate films that are formulaic. Ironically, they are usually the only ones! Not that we don't look for interesting plots and twists. The truth is that, although the scope of human experience is finite, our imagination is limitless!

So there is plenty of opportunity to change, alter, and modify scene, setting, time and dialog (think of how many times Shakespeare has been done and redone successfully). I am not saying that you can't experiment for your own amusement, but that this book is about getting your deal done and there are some things about film that you should not experiment with if you want to sell or get your project financed. Keep in mind that the audience is a stakeholder in the film and therefore if a film does not deliver on their expectation, it's to its own peril.

The big 'No! No!' in project development is messing with story structure. While this book is not designed to teach story structure, it is extremely important that the filmmaker (writer, director, producer etc.) understands it, appreciates it, and applies it. There are many ways to receive a "PASS" (Rejection) from a Creative Executive at a Studio, Production Company, Agency, or Investor, but poor story structure is the number one reason for script rejection!

That might seem elementary for seasoned writers and I understand that, but experience alone does not guarantee getting a deal done.

Regardless of experience, until you have your first project sold it's a good idea to learn as much as you can about story structure! Donna M Anderson's book *The 1-3-5 Story Structure Made Simple System* is an excellent resource for helping filmmakers with story structure. And I highly recommend it!

This subject is placed here at the beginning for a reason: trying to sell a bad, ill-conceived, poorly-structured idea is a waste of time and money! Ultimately it will not and should not pass the filter — if it does, then the filmmaker and the investor alike will be in trouble.

Recently I was having lunch with a Creative Executive (CE) friend of mine and she was relating a story about a new writer who had called her production company trying to telephone pitch a script she wrote. My friend said that before she would listen to the pitch she had one question for the caller: What film school did you attend? The caller confessed that she had not attended film school yet. Needless to say, that the conversation did not move forward.

Now, this is not to suggest that film school is a must for success — all you have to think about is Steven

Spielberg's rise to fame to know that film school may be only one path to stardom. Remember Spielberg is a GENIUS, and not very many can claim that rarity. What my friend was suggesting by the application of her filter (I'm not endorsing it either way) was that it is more common for people to have a great idea for a story than it is for someone to possess the ability to WRITE a great story.

Keep in mind that the asset (Intellectual Property or IP) you are selling is not your idea but your written script! And that is what investors will invest in!

Chapter 1

What Every Filmmaker Should Know About Film Finance

Like myself, many film financiers don't know a damn thing about making a movie (unless they are also a director or producer), but we do know a hell of a lot about making money!

Conversely, filmmakers know a lot about making films but most have avoided "B" school like the plague, as if it would zap their creative energy like kryptonite.

Our goal is to bridge the knowledge gap and introduce film-school to business-school. Sort of like MFA (Masters in Fine Arts) meets MBA (Masters in Business Administration) and creates MFMBA.

One of the first things you should know about money is that it is opportunistic; that is to say money seeks opportunities to invest. Idle money may be patient but not content.

In-order to get a deal done these days we (meaning filmmakers and film financiers) need to learn to speak the same language in order to get on the same page.

After all, a filmmaker may romanticize the idea of creating a critically acclaimed artistic expression, but we all know there will be no romance without finance!

It has been my experience that many filmmakers are not familiar with the various types of financing available and what the requirements are. For example, when I managed Entertainment Banking for Union Bank in Beverly Hills, we were bombarded with calls from filmmakers who mistakenly believed that all they had to do was make an appointment, come in and pitch their project, and — voila — they got a loan! And, mind you, these were not people unfamiliar with the business; in fact, I have had numerous discussions with Academy Award winning actors who had no clue how film finance worked! This lack of familiarity wasn't their fault; after-all, they went to acting school not business school!

So now we are going to break down the different stages of film production and identify the likely sources of financing.

Making a film can be compared to building a house, and thus film-finance can be likened to the construction industry.In both industries, you are building a project: one made from Real Property (Construction) and the

Table 1

Construction	Film Finance
Architect	Writer
Plans	Script
Contractor / Developer	Executive Producer
Subcontractors	Contract Labor
Owner	Producer / Distributor Studio
Construction Loan	Production Financing
Budget / Drawdown Schedule	Budget / Drawdown Schedule
Permanent Takeout Lender	Negative Pick Up Commitment / Minimum Guarantee

other Intellectual Property (Filmmaking).

Additionally, both industries have risk. Sometimes plans that look good on paper may go awry on the job-site. Think about every visitor who has gone to the famous Winchester House in San Jose, California and asked: what the hell was the builder thinking? Similarly, many a moviegoer who has tortured him or herself by watching the epic Ishtar has probably asked the same question of the director!

At each stage of the building process money is needed to get the project closer to completion. The following are the stages of film-finance and the likely financiers/investors.

As you can see from the bellow illustration, the Filmmaker usually has to finance the early stage of development.

Figure 1-0-1
Sources of Financing

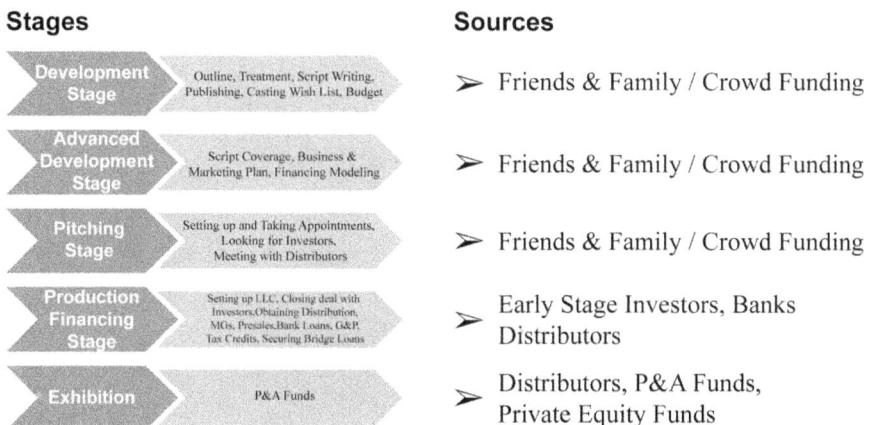

Stages   **Sources**

Stage	Description	Source
Development Stage	Outline, Treatment, Script Writing, Publishing, Casting Wish List, Budget	➤ Friends & Family / Crowd Funding
Advanced Development Stage	Script Coverage, Business & Marketing Plan, Financing Modeling	➤ Friends & Family / Crowd Funding
Pitching Stage	Setting up and Taking Appointments, Looking for Investors, Meeting with Distributors	➤ Friends & Family / Crowd Funding
Production Financing Stage	Setting up LLC, Closing deal with Investors, Obtaining Distribution, MGs, Presales, Bank Loans, G&P, Tax Credits, Securing Bridge Loans	➤ Early Stage Investors, Banks Distributors
Exhibition	P&A Funds	➤ Distributors, P&A Funds, Private Equity Funds

3

DEVELOPMENT STAGE: Outline, Treatment, Script Writing, Script Polishing, Budget Preparation, Casting Wish List, Business Plan Writing, Story Boarding.

ADVANCE DEVELOPMENT: Script Coverage, Marketing Plan Development, Financial Modeling, Pay or Play Advances.

PITCHING STAGE: Making appointments, looking for investors, talking to banks, seeking Distribution.

FINANCING STAGE: Setting up LLC, Closing deal with investors, obtaining a Minimum Guarantee, Presales, Obtaining a Negative Pickup from Distributor, Obtaining a Bank Loan, Getting Gap Financing, Finishing Funds, Lining up Tax Credits and securing a Bridge Loan. And finally, securing P & A (Prints and Ad's) funds.

There are different types of financing arrangements such as debt, equity, trade, tax credits and tax rebates. Each type has its own risks and rewards.

Debt, for the most part, is a loan and is expected to be repaid first with little if any risk of default. In the film finance world, debt is the safest level while equity the riskiest part of the financing pyramid.

Figure 1-0-2

Film Financing Pyramid

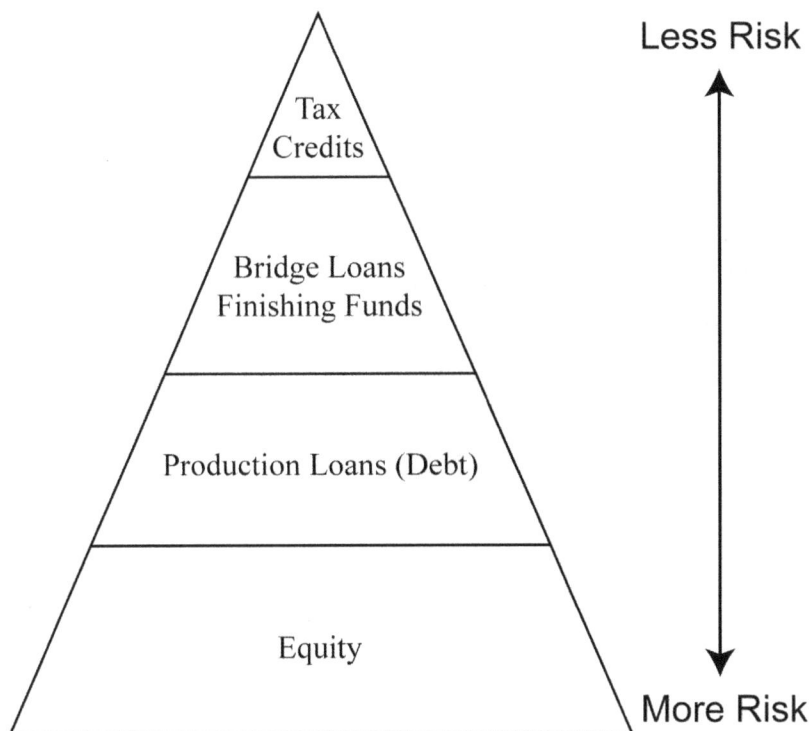

There is a finance theory called the Risk Return Premium. It simply means that the higher the risk and longer the term, the more unpredictable a project becomes and more skeptical the investor will be; hence the more they should expect to make.

In Business School, students are taught that risk should be measured in terms of how close the investment can be compared to US Treasury securities. US Treasury securities are considered the safest (given the US's current fiscal situation I can understand why you might want to laugh out loud) investments in the world.

Investment Risk Profile

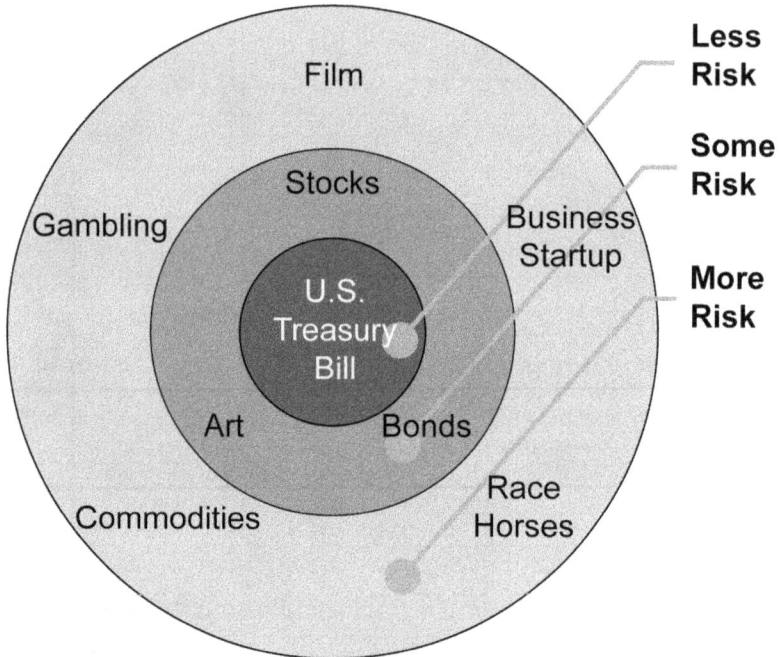

Film

Less
Risk

Stocks

Some
Risk

Gambling

Business
Startup

U.S.
Treasury
Bill

More
Risk

Art   Bonds

Race
Horses

Commodities

The further you get from the most predictable investment, as far as repayment of principal is concerned, the riskier an investment looks. As you can see from this chart, filmmaking is on the outer edge of risk.

The reason film is considered high-risk is understandable and regrettable at the same time. One reason for this is that the world of film finance is a small, and therefore highly misunderstood, business. The lack of transparency and a dubious history of some folks getting burned accounts for a lot of distrust and fear. That, coupled with the fact that a bad idea plus a horrible script, subpar directing, topped off with a heap of uneducated money, makes a lethal cocktail!

The recent history of film finance is replete with the gold-rush mentality of fools and shysters. For example, in the 1980's, large Insurance Companies jumped in and guaranteed not only to protect the investors' principal equity but also their profits! It was unbelievable, and everybody and their mother wanted to help the insurance companies out of their cash before the jig was up! It ended with the predictable finger (middle) pointing and protracted lawsuits and another financing source biting the dust!

Then, in the 1990s, it was the German Pension Funds that provided a tax incentive to direct retirement money to film finance. This, too, led to massive fraud and equally massive losses.

In the 2000's it was the Hedge Funds turn to get burned. They used their MBA's from the best schools in the country and their highly leveraged money and fueled an incredible amount of bad movie production because there was too much money chasing lesser quality projects and everybody, again, wanted in on the action. What seemed like a walk in the park for the young, smart and talented masters of the universe, turned out to be a mugging! Some were arrogant, some were stupid, and most were blind.

Unfortunately, all these financing schemes have the same characteristics: greed and fear, which led to drought and famine. And the result is that filmmakers have had to constantly scramble for new sources of financing.

The purpose of this random walk down memory lane is to help you understand the back-story that explains why finding financing is the most difficult part of the business. If, in the past, investors had consistently gotten their money back and turned a reasonable profit, we would not be having this conversation! Hopefully this helps explain investor skittishness.

My colleagues and I believe that chasing uneducated money is wrong and unsustainable. More importantly, there is a better way! As advisers, our ultimate goal is to educate money sources by bringing discipline and transparency to the film-finance conversation.

Sure, as long as the film business has a low barrier of entry it will attract sociopaths and other bad actors who don't give a damn about raping, robbing, and pillaging the naïve.

But dream with me for a moment: what if there was a legitimate, steady stream of funds for worthy (we will define worthy later) projects that provided investors with protection and reduced film finance to normal risk, comparable with other investments, and, at the same time allowed filmmakers all over the world to compete for access to funding from a large pool of investors without territorial boundaries? This is the new world we are entering made possible by the Internet!

People get in the filmmaking and film-finance

businesses for different reasons. Some are attracted to the mystique of the power film has over our cultural psyche. Others are attracted to the potential for high returns. Still others want to hangout with talent and party like rock-stars. Then there're those who couldn't make it to superstardom on one side of the camera but found a new and much richer life on the other side (think the iconic Aaron Spelling).

Regardless of your personal reasons, one thing is for sure: no one gets in this business to lose money! The best way not to lose, and give yourself and your investor a chance to win, is by reducing risk.

The following are a few key ways risk can be substantially reduced and make your project standout!

WATCH for trends in the marketplace. An old proverb says that there is nothing new under the Sun. And this is acutely true in the movie business! Hot genres (think Horror) are cyclical. Today it maybe big Tent Pole projects that are based on comic book characters, tomorrow it maybe action or thrillers.

The problem is that when something is hot it attracts a lot of attention which eventually leads to saturation which then leads to audience fatigue. The end result is lackluster box office performance and massive losses.

Evolutionary Psychologists theorize that films reflect our basic needs of Love, Good vs. Evil, Greed, Fear, Salvation, Redemption, Retribution, Adventure, and Hope. Keep in mind: it takes about 18 months from the beginning of production to reach the screen. Because of this long sales cycle, you need to be careful that your project is not behind the taste curve.

RESEARCH is unbelievably important. Research is everything! Not just the talent, but also the budget and the elements. Don't fool yourself in believing or trying to sell an investor by comparing your action film to a James Bond movie! There is only one James Bond and unless you own Sony or MGM you don't have one!

So many filmmakers make this mistake and lose all credibility by cherry-picking comparables that have no relevance or are statistical outliers that are seldom if ever repeated! Selling is not over-promised hype.

ANALYSIS is simply taking a hard ,objective look at your project and subjecting it to outside scrutiny. When you do your financial modeling, make sure it can be validated! Promising high double-digit returns just to appeal to an investor's greed usually fails miserably. If you have done a great job in the writing and packaging of your project, you should not fear criticism.

In addition to professional script coverage, you should have your budget reviewed by an experienced line-producer and perhaps a Completion Bond Insurance Company. They will tell you if you have a competitive project and whether it can be completed within budget. Worst-case scenario is that you will be told the truth and be free to move on to a better idea and not waste your time or your investors money!

I don't want to instill doubt in your pet project, but all too often filmmakers fall in love with the wrong thing.

While investor's first love is money, a filmmaker's first love is often his or her own passion. You need both, but money trumps passion.

Likewise, preparing Financial Ultimates (projections & cash flows) helps an investor translate your ideas into a language he or she can understand. This is a critical step! Yes: to do this right, it will require some investment by you but *for* you; it will set you apart from your competitors and give your potential investors a higher comfort level!

PACKAGING is not about some slick Photoshop presentation; it is, however, about substance. It's having a well thought-out and researched proposal that includes all of the above along with marketing strategies and distribution commitments and talent attachements.

Having the right talent attached is critical, but not just faces and names: the value-added component of talent. For instance, lets say you have a very popular star's name attached to the project (because you have an inside hookup) that has been in a number of big time box office successes -- does that really translate into sales for your project? Could their success have been because they were paired correctly? Have they ever played a leading role without additional star power? How much value did they add to the revenue stream? This can be measured and is not just notional because they were apart of all-star cast. You should definitely make sure the value-added component is a part of your package.

When a good friend and business partner of mine,

Tim Story, and producer Will Packer and their team were selecting the cast for his movie *Think Like A Man*, consideration was given to the Social Media followers potential cast members had. They were able to cleverly leverage social media to get butts in seats and it worked remarkably!

If you include all these risk-mitigants, you will be well on your way to funding, and it's a **WRAP** for your project!

CHAPTER 2

How Much Is A Shot At Your Dreams Worth?

If you knew in advance that your hard work would payoff by allowing you to realize your dreams, what would you, in present time, be willing to invest in order to make that dream come true?

This is not merely a thought exercise but a basic tenant of manifest destiny! Perhaps you may be like me in that you have never been lucky. I have not won even a crackerjack prize! So I don't rely on luck; instead, I have learned many times the hard way that the old work ethos is true: 'Plan the work, work the plan, and be prepared to rework the plan.'

The point is, in order to realize success, you have to be prepared to invest in yourself before you can expect someone else — especially a stranger — to invest in you!

Some filmmakers believe that the only thing they have to do is to come up with an idea, write a script, hard-sell the idea to someone, let Lady Luck do her thing, and enjoy the riches and fame!

As nice as that sounds, it's a bigger fantasy than the story they wrote about!

True: you do have to nail down all the preliminary stuff, but that's just the beginning.

Hollywood is replete with great stories and scripts that have never been seen!

One of the reasons is exposure. Not that the project was not exposed, but perhaps not to the right person or audience or in the right way.

I remember in college I was very excited about a paper I wrote and wanted to get some feedback (read: praise) from one of my favorite professors. As he began to peruse my work he abruptly handed it back to me. Stupid me asked "So what did you think about my concept?" he said, "I didn't think anything." I asked "Why?" He said there was so many grammatical errors it blocked his brain from getting to the concept!

Needless to say my embarrassment exceeded my initial excitement! The lesson then is still valid now; your project has to be as tight as you can make it before anyone will see your vision!

We all want the widest exposure we can get but if not seen by the right audience in the right way at the right time, we are just wasting time!

So back to the question at hand: Are we prepared to invest in our project and ourselves? And I don't mean just time! I mean money. Not a lot of money, but a little money? I make this point here because our social media outlets have conditioned us with a misconception of "free." The real problem is that is has created an expectation of "free" that is inconsistent with the notion of "you get what you pay for!" Everybody pays, either with their attention, their information, or their cash.

This has led to the old adage of *"Fee* For Service" being replaced by a new mindset of *"Free* For Service."

To illustrate this issue is a recent conversation I had with a filmmaker. I was telling him about our new online film finance platform that matched filmmakers with financiers and he said "Wow, what a great idea! Sign me up!" I then went on to tell him that there was a modest (Under $30.00) monthly subscription fee to cover servicing costs. Suddenly his demeanor changed and he became very inquisitive, asking if there was a guarantee. Not a completely unreasonable question, but thats like asking Match.com if they guarantee marriage! Mind you, he was all for it until he realized he had to pay! I need say nothing more; you know the type.

Many filmmakers (and wannabes) spend precious time (theirs; ours) and money trying to get mostly uninterested people to listen to their pitch. They hope that their persuasive powers can reach beyond their writing ability and into someone else's pocket. Sometime this works and sometimes it doesn't.

The old paradigm is to have you, the filmmaker, run around town pitching your project to anyone willing to listen.

You may spend countless hours trying to get a hookup or leveraging someone else's hookup. After all, we have all been taught in the film business "it's all about who you know," right? Wrong!

What if you could save all that time and money? What if you could be more efficient with your time, energy and resource?   What if the paradigm shifted under your feet like a 9.0 California earthquake? What if you now possessed the power to change the game from the antiquated "who you know" to "who knows you"? Would you invest (not just spend) in yourself to allow your dreams the widest and biggest opportunity to be realized?

For most folks the short answer is "hell yes!" But how can you get the most bang for your precious buck? Herein lies the entire premise of **Online Film Financing from professional sources**.

I beg you not to get this twisted. Yes I am trying to sell you something; I am trying to sell you — YOU!

Let me walk you through it. But first, ask yourself this question: would you prefer to have investors, distributors, and bankers come to you or would you rather chase them down like a stalker and beg them for a meeting?

The answer is obvious. Here's how we (yes we, as in US, WE, You & I) are going to make that a reality!

Professional use of the Internet allows filmmakers to connect with funding sources like never before. I won't at this point talk about Crowd Funding (see Chapter 12); I'm talking about Online Professional Funding.

Figure 2-0-3

New Paradigm

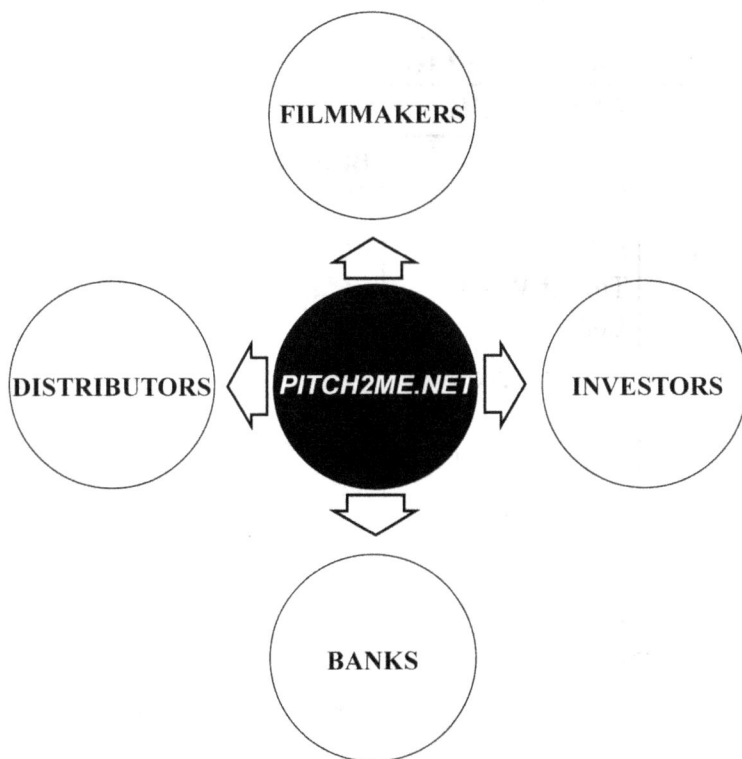

As you can see in Figure 2-0-3, there is a way to bring professional film financiers together with filmmakers. This central marketspace allows all the players to be at the same table at the same time connecting creative ideas, opportunities, access and cash. This will facilitate getting deals done in a more efficient and timely manner.

Within this marketspace, all the pertinent questions about a potential project can be answered. Most film financiers have very specific questions they need answered in order to evaluate and propose a financing structure that works for them. Here is a partial list of things a financier needs to know or have access to in this evaluation process:

Information Needed to Make Financial Decision			
PERSONAL	**CREATIVE**	**FINANCIAL**	**LEGAL**
Bio's Director Producer Writer Film School	Script/ Synopsys/ Treatment Talent Wish-List Script Coverage Sizzle Reel/ Teaser/Trailer Story Board Log Line Location Genre Language Type of Release CIRCA	Budget(Top Sheet) Marketing Plan Business Plan FBIndex™ Financial Ultimates Sales Agent Pre Sales Sales Estimates Minimum Guarantee (MG) Type of Financing Required Proof of Funds (POF)	Copyright Certificate Number Chain of Title Legal Entity (SPE)

Additionally, filmmakers are able to upload a 2-minute direct pitch to all investors via video.

On the investor side, any potential investor, banker, distributor is able to browse any project and sort by budget, genre, MPAA rating, FBIndex™, subject, project completeness, percent of financing already obtained, type of financing required etc.

What if, after all this, investors still show you no love? Thank them! They did you a huge favor and silently told you to keep it moving and move on up to something better! It's like that old boyfriend or girlfriend that isn't getting any better even though you put a lot of work into them — NEXT!

Overall, pitching online makes all the sense in the world. It allows filmmakers access to capital (in any form) and allows serious film financer's access to projects ready for financing.

We have now planned the work, now it is up to you to *work the plan!*

Chapter 3

What A Good Pitch Looks Like

Back to business school! A good pitch is a short version of a business model. A good business model will always contain these elements:

Table 2

Business Model	
"B" School	**"F" School**
Customer Selection	Audience / Genre / Rating
Scope	Distribution Medium (DVD, Theatrical, International)
Differentiation	POV (Point of View)
Value Recapture	Return (ROI, IRR)

It has been said that a great pitch(er) should:

- Be Prepared,
  - Be Brief,
    - Be Seated.

BE PREPARED

No one knows your project better than you! However, sometimes the words you need to convey it can escape you. That is why, unless you are Allen Iverson, you need to **PRACTICE! PRACTICE! PRACTICE!**

We are not talking about just practicing in front of the proverbial mirror (although this can help); we are talking about practicing in front of those who will brutally but honestly offer you a helpful critique!

Most of us are familiar with Broadway in New York. It's where stage plays are catapulted into iconic success or banished into obscurity. There is a huge lesson to be learned here. Smart money says before you debut on Broadway you should practice your shtick **OFF BROADWAY!**

In other words, don't practice your pitch in front of potential investors. By the time you are talking to investors, you better have your pitch down pat! Get the kinks out before you get kicked out!

If, after you have practiced your pitch and you are still not feeling it, hire some else to do it for you. This step is not preferred but think about TV Commercials: the actors are not owners but no one can doubt their effectiveness. The point is, you may only get one shot at a potential investor. There will be not second round if you get knocked out in the first.

BE BRIEF

Very few people are blessed with the patience of Job (as in the Bible). In fact, most of us — at one time or another — have suffered from ADD! This is especially true of investors! They are as impatient as their money.

Brevity is as difficult for some as patience is for others; this is why practice is essential. No one (except Lawyers) makes money by taking meetings.

So, when you develop your pitch, make sure you hit the highlights and, as on Broadway, make them so engaged that they are left begging for more!

We don't want to oversell our project and end up underselling our credibility. Remember: the pitch is just a teaser for your project. If we have done a great job putting together a compelling project that exceeds investor's expectations, then our pitch should be just as compelling and just as credible.

BE SEATED

This is not easy! I remember once I was on a sales call with my boss. I have always considered myself a salesman, even if the only product I was selling was myself. This time, however, although I felt I was on a roll, my boss later informed me when we were debriefing the call, that she saw things different. When asked for her thoughts she said "Well, I thought for a while you were doing pretty good, but I think it would have been better if you had stopped a few paragraphs earlier!" She was spot on!

So never mistake politeness for patience or interest!

Brevity enables the investor to absorb your idea and formulate questions and allow you time to answer them. Since questions are a sign of interest it should take up more time than the pitch itself.

Being prepared is not just being glib. It means that you understand and respect your audience: respect their time, their opinion, and their decisions.

Even if you are well prepared, well rehearsed, appropriately brief, and know when to take your seat when the music stops, not every investor is going to write you a check. Don't take it personally! Your job is to be ready and get your project in front of enough potential investors.

How does this work online? If you visit a crowd funding site, you see pitches that are all over the place! While I am not aware of any scientific study about whose campaign succeeds based on their type of pitch, I know one thing: when it comes to professional funders, begging does not have a high success rate.

A professional financier is interested in the product, opportunity, risk, and reward. Since, when you pitch online, a potential investor does not initially have the opportunity to ask questions (most questions can be answered by the material on your profile) they will want to know who you are as a person and filmmaker. If they like what they see then they will contact you to setup a personal meeting. When you get to an in-person meeting, the rules change a bit because different skills, such as building one-on-one rapport, listening, and asking appropriate questions, will be needed. There is actually a time-tested sequence for in-person pitch meetings that is germane to Hollywood. In any case, even though the medium may change, the above rules will still apply!

CHAPTER 4

How Does The Cash Flow In Film Finance?

One thing you can count on when it comes to money: it has behavioral issues. This is because each deal is truly different. There is nothing standard about film finance.

The reason for this is because, depending on the Budget, Genre, Rating, Deal Points, etc, revenues come from different sources. For example, suppose your project doesn't have enough P & A funds — you will most likely go direct to DVD and have no foreign sales.

Another example: suppose your Genre is that of a cultural minority, and that groups' experience is germane only to the host country, it would be unlikely that you would receive international acceptance because it may lack universally recognized themes. This means that audiences abroad cannot relate nor emotionally connect with your POV. On the other hand, this same challenge could be overcome by making a documentary instead of a feature film.

Therefore if you remove the international element of the cash flow waterfall then you will be relying strictly on host country domestic theatrical or direct to DVD sales. In territories such as Africa, South America, and parts of the Middle East, the main distribution is via DVD sales, as there is no mature exhibition facilities (This is not true of, say, China).

There is no cookie-cutter way to illustrate all the potential variables of waterfalls. The following diagram lays out the broad stokes for an internationally released film that had the international rights sold.

The figure that follows takes the diagram and puts numbers behind it. It illustrates typical expenses and

Revenue Flow Chart

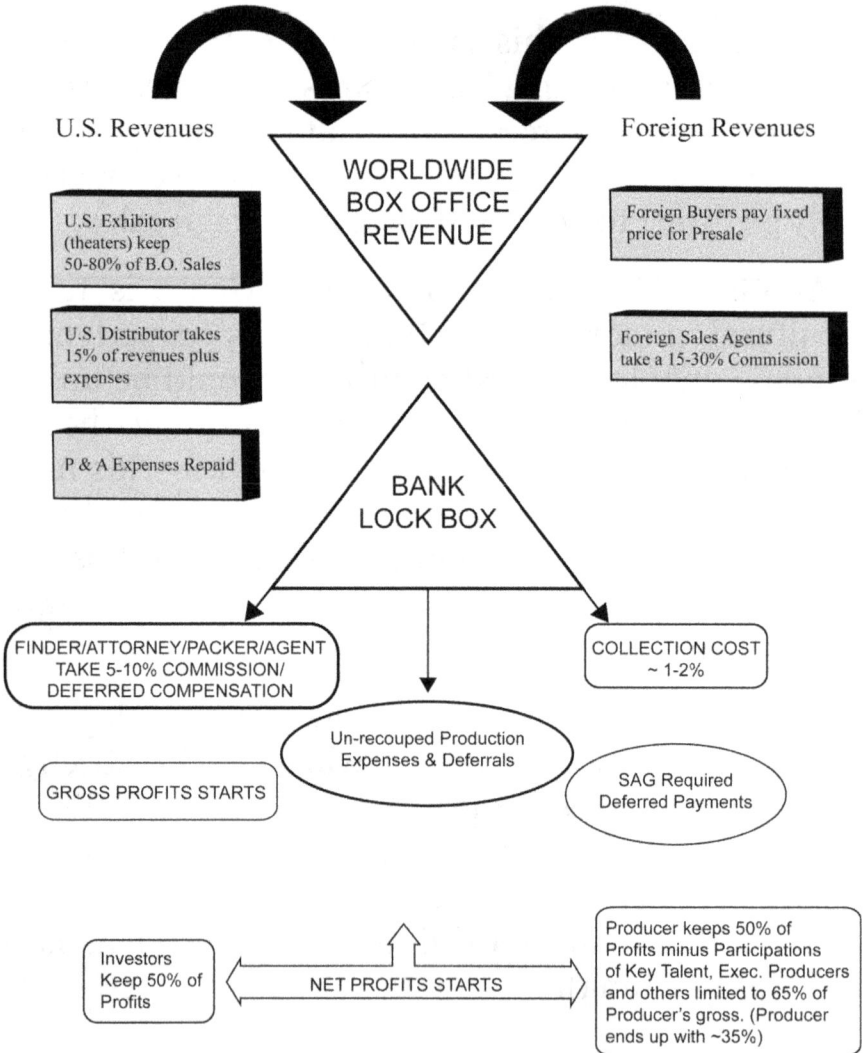

U.S. Revenues

Foreign Revenues

WORLDWIDE BOX OFFICE REVENUE

U.S. Exhibitors (theaters) keep 50-80% of B.O. Sales

Foreign Buyers pay fixed price for Presale

U.S. Distributor takes 15% of revenues plus expenses

Foreign Sales Agents take a 15-30% Commission

P & A Expenses Repaid

BANK LOCK BOX

FINDER/ATTORNEY/PACKER/AGENT TAKE 5-10% COMMISSION/ DEFERRED COMPENSATION

COLLECTION COST ~ 1-2%

Un-recouped Production Expenses & Deferrals

GROSS PROFITS STARTS

SAG Required Deferred Payments

Investors Keep 50% of Profits

NET PROFITS STARTS

Producer keeps 50% of Profits minus Participations of Key Talent, Exec. Producers and others limited to 65% of Producer's gross. (Producer ends up with ~35%)

revenue corridors. Remember: not all deals will be structured this way but most likely will each deal will have similar components.

Figure 4-0-1

Typical Revenue Cash Flows (for illustrative purposes only)

Gross Revenues

U.S. Box Office Revenue		$	45,000,000.00
Less Exhibitors 60% Share	60%	$	27,000,000.00
U.S. Distributors Share 40%	40%	$	18,000,000.00
Ancillary (DVD, TV, Pay, Cable, Etc.)		$	67,500,000.00
Less U.S. Distribution Fee	15%	$	12,825,000.00
Domestic (U.S.) Sales Agents Fee	10%	$	1,800,000.00
P & A Expense		$	23,000,000.00
Net from U.S. Box & Ancillary		$	47,875,000.00
Foreign Buyer Set Price		$	13,500,000.00
Foreign Sales Agent Fee	15%	$	2,025,000.00
Packager / Agent / Attorney Commission	5%	$	675,000.00
Collector	1%	$	135,000.00
Foreign Net		$	10,665,000.00
Gross Profits		$	58,540,000.00
S.A.G Required Deferred Payments to Talent			
Investor Recoupment	115%	$	34,500,000.00
Un-recouped Expenses & Defferals	1%	$	300,000.00
Net Profits		$	23,740,000.00
Investors 50%	50%	$	11,870,000.00
Production Company 50%	50%	$	11,870,000.00
Key Participants (25%)	25%	$	2,967,500.00
Executive Producers & Co-Producer	25%	$	2,967,500.00
Other Professionals	15%	$	1,780,500.00
Producers Portion	35%	$	4,154,500.00

Assumptions

U.S. B.O.=125% of BUD	$	45,000,000.00
Net Budget-Incentives	$	30,000,000.00
Foreign set price 30% U.S.	$	13,500,000.00
U.S. Screens	$	2,300.00
P & A	$	23,000,000.00
Ancillary DVD, TV, Pay, Ect.	$	67,500,000.00

Revenue Timeline

Time from Negotiations to Cash-flow: Aproximately 24 Months

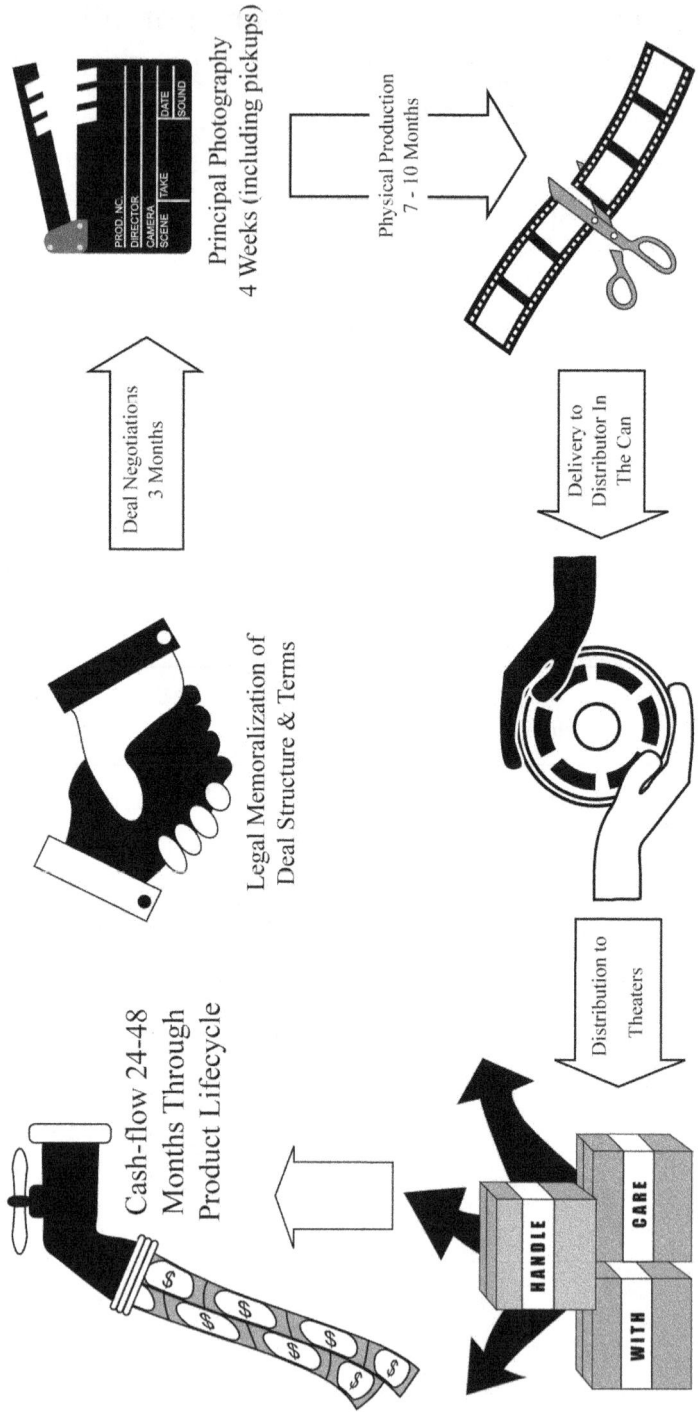

Principal Photography
4 Weeks (including pickups)

Physical Production
7 - 10 Months

Deal Negotiations
3 Months

Legal Memoralization of
Deal Structure & Terms

Delivery to
Distributor In
The Can

Distribution to
Theaters

HANDLE CARE WITH

Cash-flow 24-48
Months Through
Product Lifecycle

It can take up to about 48 months to start seeing returns (post recoupment of budget) for your project. If you plan to sell your project at a film festival then you may be able to shorten the cash-flow cycle. On the other hand, you are going to need some very patient investors.

Typically you will be making the principal and profit back from DVD, (and now mainly) Rental (Netflix, Redbox, BLOCKBUSTER) and Foreign sales. We look at Theatrical release as advertising for home video. This is not to say that it's impossible to make positive cash-flow from the box office; but, given the cost of P & A plus distributions and other fees, it is more likely that you will see free cash later in the collection cycle.

CHAPTER 5

Investors: Should You Fear Film Finance?

A little fear is always healthy. It can serve as a check to an overblown ego and allow us to stay rational. But fear is usually born out of a lack understanding; the more we know the less we fear.

Investors, by definition, are risk-takers, but they want to take risks that they understand and can manage.

So at this point, our goal is to demystify the world of film finance. Because there is no governing body, except tradition and creativity, as to how films are financed, there is an understandable level of trepidation as to how to structure and manage the risk of a film deal.

Previously, we have outlined the risks associated with film finance, but there are plenty of rewards that balance out that risk.

Film deals usually have higher returns than other types of investments; have long-term residual revenues, and create significant library value. As an example, you should expect to receive between 15-25% returns depending on which financial vehicle and structure you choose. Each stage of financing has its own return characteristics.

The following are example of financing types and the expected returns.

Table 3

Typical Funding Options

Type	Expected Return	Risk	Repayment Hierarchy
P & A Funds	15-18%	5	1
Finishing Funds	25-30%	3	1
Bridge Loans	20%	7	1
Gap	20-30%	2	3
Tax Incentives	10-20%	7	1
Negative Pick Up	Libor + 3	7	1
Mezzanine	15-20%	1	5
Equity / Development	18-25%	1	5

Scale: 1= High Risk 7= Low Risk   Repayment 1= High Priority 5=Lower Priority

Returns are influenced (if not dictated) by a number of factors such as: proximity to cash, liquidity, timing of return of principal, and risk of default.

All of the financing types listed in the above table, except for P & A (Prints and Ad's), are monies used in the development or production of the project before it is publicly released.

FINISHING FUNDS are usually needed after principal production is completed and there is a need for additional money for items such as pickup shots (additional photography) or soundtrack completion that was not included in original budget or exceeds reserves. Finishing funds are considered small (relative to the budget) short-term loans and are paid back out of reserves when the film is delivered (In The Can) to the distributor.

BRIDGE LOANS are very short-term loans that serve as a financing bridge between the producer needing to get the project started and Negative Pickup loans. For example, say the bank has agreed to make the loan but it's going to take them 30 to 60 days to document and secure everything; but you the producer need money now to pay talent or secure locations or face losing Pay or Play money you have previously advanced to Talent. Bridge Loans are usually only a small fraction of the total budget. The risk profile of bridge loans can be very low if done right.

GAP financing is the difference between the budget and the guaranteed minimum, or Negative Pickup (Negative means the film negative delivered to the distributor) It usually relies on foreign sales estimates to determine value and foreign sales contracts for repayment. Usually the risk is embedded in the fact that the foreign sales are not, in this case, pre-sold on the credit-standing of the sales agent. The reason for this arbitrage is that when a film project is not pre-sold, a producer can ask for a higher sales price because the quality and marketability of the film can be determined with a higher degree of certainty after it is completed rather than before it is completed. It's like making a marriage proposal before a blind date.

TAX INCENTIVES are offered by States (or Countries) to attract film production as a means to stimulate their economies and train their workforce. They usually come in two forms: Credits, which are deductions against expenses and are usually sold to qualifying local residents, and Tax Rebates. Rebates come directly from the governing agency and do not have to be sold to residents and are therefore preferable. There is marginal risk in this type of financing; however, you have to be diligent about what specific items are allowed and/or disavowed as well as the credit-standing of the governing agency.

NEGATIVE PICKUPS suffer from a confusing name! It has nothing to do with losses or deficits. It simply means the film negative (as in Cellulose Photography) being picked up by the distributor.

Before the film goes into production, a distributor may issue a guarantee to pay a fixed amount (budget) if the finished film contains all the agreed-upon elements.

Usually a bank will finance (at a discount to budget or guarantee) the production and, when it's finished, the distributor will pay off the bank loan and take delivery. Typically there is relatively not much risk in this area of financing because there is a lot of oversight by insurance bond companies and others. However, if the distributor files for bankruptcy or suffers from severe cash-flow problems, they may delay or default on commitments.

MEZZANINE FINANCING (Mezz) is a fancy term that means that it is just above the equity financier. It's like the floor just above floor 1 in the elevator. However, it has some interesting characteristics. It behaves like a loan and equity at the same time. Usually it's a debt that can be converted into equity if the project hits certain milestones or roadblocks.

EQUITY is the most critical part of the film financing structure. It has the most risk and the most upside rewards. Equity is usually the hardest to raise because it takes the longest to get repaid and it has the highest degree of uncertainty. It runs on a cash flow hierarchy principal we will call First In Last Out (FILO). However, the risk associated with equity can be mitigated when properly assessed and structured.

Now that we have discussed the various financing options, lets revisit whether or not film finance is as scary as some of the horror stories you may have heard!

Arguably, one of the worst film finance stories in history is that of the *Cleopatra* film project. Back in 1963 Fox agreed to finance this epic that had an original budget of $2 million dollars. After many talent and director changes, that budget swelled to $47 million dollars (about $340 million in 2010 dollars, ranking #3 all time) before it all was said and done! And at least a few of us have heard the urban legend of FOX having to sell its back lot (what is now Century City) to save it from bankruptcy. Anecdotally, this critically defamed bomb won four (4) academy awards and was the highest grossing film of the year! But the most important lesson we can draw here is that eventually all the debt was paid and the film made back all its cost!

The unknown truth is that most films that are theatrically released (the jury is still out for Waterworld, and Sahara) eventually make their money back! **The key is living long enough (or being immortal); you may not see any money but your grandkids will!**

Seriously, if a film project is done right, it poses no greater risk than most other alternative investments. The challenge is defining **DONE RIGHT!**

We are not just talking about the creative aspects of the project, but also the financing aspects. Most independent films are not subject to much scrutiny. We suggest the following ways to mitigate risk and reduce fear:

• Have a professional conduct Script Coverage;

• Have a respected line producer validate the budget;

• Hold the producers feet to that budget!

• Make sure the project falls within the "sweet spot" of historically profitable film budgets;

• Demand that validated Financial Ultimates be made available;

• Require an FBIndex™ (a Risk Assessment Profile);

• Depending on budget, require Presales with a reputable Sales Agent;

- Validate any proffered guarantees;
- Demand regular written financial updates and audits;
- Secure P & A funds ASAP;
- Optimize Tax Incentives;
- Do not risk any money you can't afford to lose.

Other Commonly Known Risk And Their Mitigants

Table 4

Risk	Mitigants
Failure or Delay in Completion and/or Delivery of Film	Completion Bond
Box Office Flop	Guranteed Contracts
Bankruptcy of Producer	Special Purpose Entity - Bankruptcy Remote
Labor Strike	Completion Bond
DSS (Difficult Star Syndrome)	Performance Bond

Chapter 6

What Does A Good Deal Look Like?

To some, it means a win/win situation where all expectations are met. To others, it may mean a zero sum game where winning becomes more of an obsession than riches. It really depends on whether you are interested in developing a relationship or just in it for a onetime transaction.

We believe that a balanced approach where you balance Greed and Fear to get to Fair.

Getting to Fair

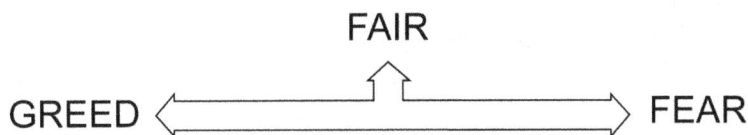

FAIR

GREED $\longleftrightarrow$ FEAR

We have all heard the popularized Wall Street mantra "Greed is Good", that may be true for a select few for a short period of time (the guy who said that went to jail), but in the long-run we have seen how greedy people have ridden the fast track from invincible to imbecile! If we are not humble we will be humiliated.

Although it may not be a popular position to take, we believe that an investor who puts in the equity component should get a disproportionate return. The typical structure is that, after an investor gets 106% to 115% of their money back, the profits are split 50/50; that is fifty percent to the investor and fifty percent to the producer (including all backend points to talent and other guild payments, etc.). The weakness in this standard structure is that it does not recognize risk.

What this requires is a true and accurate understanding of the risk and the rewards associated with your particular project. Earlier, we discussed the various types of financing schemes employed over the years to finance films. Now we need to wrap our minds around properly setting our expectations when we are in the process of negotiating a deal.

We all want the Utopian Dream; that is to have a deal that is GOOD, CHEAP, AND FAST! However, in the film business, this trifecta is close to being impossible! Why? Lets breakdown the model to understand it better.

GOOD

A good deal depends on perspective. For a producer it means that there is a fair distribution of profits and power. It's a situation that allows them an opportunity to advance their career, fame, and fortune. It also allows them creative and financial control.

From an investor point of view, it's good when there is a clear exit strategy in place before the deal is cut. It also requires that the returns are commensurate with the risk involved. And, finally, investors are wary of surprises.

FAST

Remember the old adage "speed kills"? This does not mean speed is a deal killer, but it will kill some of your returns. Cost goes up with speed. For example, you may have to hire additional lawyers to memorialize the deal. If a deal goes down fast it has to leapfrog other deals that may have been ahead of it or it requires the investor to stop what they are working on and devote extra time to your deal. Speed also creates additional costs because in the haste to get a deal done there are critical deal points that may go unresolved or unidentified.

CHEAP

We have already discussed some of the reasons cost can go up but there are others. There is a cost premium when desperation sets in. This is not unique to the film industry. Hard Money is available for almost any enterprise. The reason it's called Hard Money is telling. It's the financier/lender of last resort, when regular money is hard to come by.

You have probably seen the Ad's on TV that have celebrities pitching overnight funding for consumer loans. These loans typically carry an interest rate of 100 to 150% annually!!! Often, these deals have huge prepayment penalties or straight won't allow you to pay it off early. For a filmmaker, this would a deal killer. These types of deals should be avoided. Usually they become an option when a filmmaker has to meet deadlines or is in a hurry to get the film in the can. And for an investor, it might take the incentive away from the filmmaker to do the best job they can.

To make sure the cost of your deal is not cost prohibitive: plan well, execute better, and avoid short-cuts.

Table 6-2

Triangle of Truth

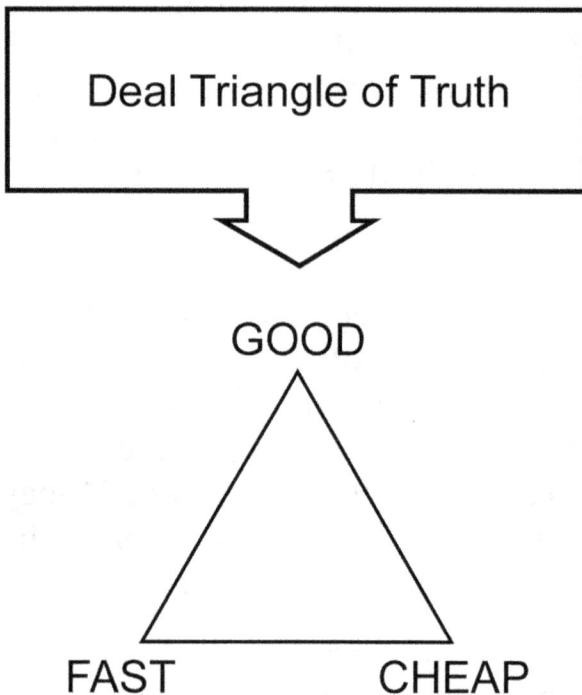

```
┌──────────────────────────────────┐
│                                  │
│   Deal Triangle of Truth         │
│                                  │
└──────────────┐      ┌────────────┘
               ↘      ↙
                 ↘  ↙
```

GOOD

```
        /\
       /  \
      /    \
     /      \
    /        \
   /          \
  /            \
 /              \
/_____\
```

FAST   CHEAP

You may select any two of the three options. One is mutually exclusive.
Key: If it is Good and Fast it will not be **Cheap**
       If it is Cheap and Good it will not be **Fast**
       If it is Fast and Cheap it will not be **Good**

Let's be honest: in the past, a number of the producers as well as others involved in the process have not treated their investors/financiers fairly. For example, you may have heard of film-funds that financed a slate of films that eventually ran into problems. Later, when the fund underperformed, it was found that the projects that went into the fund were the result of cherry picking (only putting higher risk profile films into the fund and keeping less riskier deals separate). This led to investors moving on and getting out of the film finance business, after having been taken advantage of. When that happens, we all lose big time! This is because for investors, unlike atheletes, short-term memory loss is not an asset when you are talking about losing money; investors remember losses longer than they remember gains.

The new paradigm requires that we all do what we say we are going to do and treat each other with respect and transparency, especially when things don't go as planned. As a filmmaker, you don't want your project to become a nightmare for your investors.

Top reasons why deals don't get done

- Most obvious: Poorly written or conceived script;
- Horrible package (including less than marketable talent/attachments);
- Terrible pitch;
- Can't find the right investor;
- Adverse economic conditions (such as recession);
- Deal points not fair;
- Limited commercial appeal;
- Projects gets neglected or lost in the maze of deal activity;
- Over Lawyer'd;

- Lack of unique ideas (has been done many times before);
- Few financial players in the market;
- Poor history of investor experience;
- More projects than can be financed prudently.

CHAPTER 7

How To Get In Front Of The Right Investor

Today, if you had an innovative idea that was based on technology and it had high potential for profits, you could go to any one of hundreds Venture Capitalist firms in Silicon Valley for startup capital. If you wanted a loan to buy a car, a boat, a house, or a plane you know where to go. But if you wanted funds to finance a worthy film project where would you go? The answer becomes harder.

This is why we need an alternative funding strategy. This is how the Internet allows the film finance business to have it's own marketplace to finance great ideas!

How would you like to get in front of the right investor who has been looking for a project just like yours? How would you do that? Until now, the only way to develop interest in your project would be to call everyone you know and try and develop interest in your project. Or you could do as Spike Lee and others once did: finance it on credit cards or on the backs of your friends and family. Or you could hop in your car a go to all the film festivals and seminars and talk to whomever will listen. Any one of these strategies might work, but, as I stated before, they are not a very efficient use of time or limited resources.

Now you can have investors seeking you out. By putting your project online, you will have access to investors who are tailored just for you all over the world! Think about it: you can cast a wide net by being specific and demonstrating a complete picture of how your project can meet the dual needs of your audience as well as the needs of the investors!

Also, you can put together not just one investor, but several at the same time. Some investors require that they will only issue a conditional commitment if you are able to line up all the other money needed to complete your budget.

Lets say that your project has an estimated budget of $500,000. And you have already raised the initial $50,000. With an online presence, you can have a project money meter that communicates to potential investors how much you have raised thus far and what is remaining to complete the budget. Any investor viewing your project page will be able to issue additional commitments until you have reached your budget. Then, the only thing left to do is close the deal and memorialize it from a legal standpoint. Investors want to know that they are not the only ones interested or in the deal; there is confidence in numbers.

The idea behind online pitching is mass customization. We want to match each project with the right investor(s); almost like some of the popular dating sites. But, more importantly, we want to maintain a steady flow of financing sources for worthy projects by making sure investors are treated fairly, rewarded properly, and return regularly.

Ways to improve your odds

There is an estimated $1.5 Trillion USD waiting on the sidelines for the right investment opportunity. But right now money for film deals is scarce. Why the contradiction? The answer is simple: investors experience discomfort in opportunities they don't understand.

The earlier chapters of this book have served to increase investor's comfort levels by educating investors and filmmakers on how deals can get done. But more is needed.

As a filmmaker, your project deserves the widest possible chance to get in front of the right finance team. A lot of money available does not negate the fact that there is serious competition for it. In 2010 there were over 10,000 movies made in the USA. Out of that number 300 were released theatrically. Of that number, only 40 were independent film projects. Draw your own conclusions.

One conclusion we all can draw is that there are more deals than real opportunity. So how do you get your deal to standout from the crowd?

First, it has to appeal to a broad audience relative to its budget. Second, it has to have a clear path to financial success. And third, it has to give an investor a level of comfort that gives them confidence that you as the filmmaker know what you are doing and you will treat them fairly.

Your audience appeal has to be proven. That is why you should have script coverage and a marketing plan that honestly demonstrates that you are on point.

It may be costly, but you need to spend the necessary resources to provide your investors with a financial scenario that protects their investment. This means a business plan that includes validate-able Financial Ultimates that are reasonably achievable. In addition, you will need to be able to answer investor questions and concerns (see list of items in Chapter 2) demonstrating your understanding of risk and what you have done to mitigate it.

You will also need to make sure that you use every technique at your disposal to ensure you are at the top of an investor's mind when it comes to funding an opportunity.

If your project is acceptable, reasonable, and profitable, you can expect that it is also fundable.

CHAPTER 8

Investors: Why Invest In Film?

Better than average returns

The most obvious answer is that there is lots of money to be made! However, that is only part of the story. Provided it is done right, film investments can act as an annuity. Our finance model is to return investor principal and consideration back in 48 months. After that, it's all gravy. It keeps on giving in perpetuity. Also, if you are financing multiple films, you are building library value that can be resold or repurposed for new technology and distribution vehicles.

Portfolio diversification

You may be a single investor managing your own portfolio or you may be a money manger for multiple clients. Whatever the case, it is your responsibility to recommended and/or research your or your client's passions. We recommend that you never invest more than you can afford to lose, or at least not more the 10% of your investible assets in film finance.

However, we believe that film finance is a viable and potentially lucrative alternative investment. It should never be the centerpiece of your portfolio just as real estate should not be. The lure of following your passions should be tempered by a well thought-out business decision.

Over the years, it has been often said that the entertainment business is recession proof. That is not necessarily true; however, the film business has been and for the foreseeable future will be cyclically neutral, in that it's a relatively inexpensive consumer experience. There is also abundant proof that it satisfies other psychological and sociological functions that prove its worth; however, the limits of time and space won't allow us to get into that at this time.

Opportunity to make cultural impact

When I visited Abu Dhabi and Dubai a few years ago, the big talk around town when it came to business was real estate; no real surprise there! However, when I spoke with the cultural ministry, the one thing they wanted help with was knowledge transfer. They wanted our firm to help create positive images of the Arab world through the medium of film. They had taken great steps to invest and create a thriving media district in the Free Zones.

There are many ways investors can, via the power of film, have impact on misunderstood or maligned groups. Obviously documentaries are a proven vehicle to accomplish this aim.

For example, some people argue that one of the foundation stones to the acceptance of a Black President of the United States was the film *Deep Impact* starring Morgan Freeman as President as well as the hit television series *24* starring Dennis Haysbert. Whether these claims are true or not, you cannot ignore how influential positives images are.

Almost everyone has a passion that they are willing to support; especially if there is a community of like-minded people. We believe that a well thought-out on-line platform will allow investors and filmmakers to unite in the pursuit of their collective interest.

Helps Build A Lifetime Legacy

Filmmaking is over 100 years old. We are still impacted by early films that have taken up residence in our National and International psyche. Whether you agree with the content or not, think about the film Birth of A Nation (I am not advocating it's message) and how powerful its symbolism was and still is! Also, let's not forget the controversial Nazi propaganda films by Leni Riefenstal. We also have the legacy of films such as *Gone With The Wind, Kramer vs. Kramer, The Color Purple, Roots* and hundreds of others that have a lasting impact on our worldview.

The point is, being part of the filmmaking/financing process allows you the opportunity to leave your own stamp on history. Just look at the explosion of YouTube™; there you can find a clip of almost any film ever made!

The unique thing about film is its lasting value and its ability to generate interest and curiosity, and oftentimes money, in perpetuity! In film, your legacy can turn into an annuity!

Chapter 9

Film Business Intelligence

While the studios have a sophisticated GREEN-LIGHT process, this is not true of the indie film world where there are no universal standards for green-lighting a project. The studios employ MBA's that run Monte Carlo simulations — intensive financial models — and, after all the analysis is completed, hand it over to a committee that at times employs outside consultants. All this is done to try and vet out and identify any risk BEFORE the GO is given.

One reason these strategies are not done in the indie world is because it is typically cost prohibitive and most independent filmmakers are not blessed with deep pockets! But this lack of resources does not negate the need for tools that will help investors safeguard their investment.

What if there was a way that an independent filmmaker or financier of independent films could have access to tools that the Big Boys And Big Girls use?

When my business partner (Brenda Doby-Flewellyn) and I first started our company (FILMBANKERS International LLC) I asked her a question: "Do you believe that there are common elements of a film project that determine success or failure?" To be honest I was really afraid of her answer! My fear stemmed from the fact that there is a natural conflict between finance and creativity. I have a curiosity and affinity toward statistics and I had an idea that we could develop a statistical model that would allow a filmmaker and/or a film financier the ability to analyze a project before it was made to assess it viability. To my surprise my partner did not shoot down my idea but just said "maybe".

With that positive (if you knew my partner Brenda you would understand that she pulls no punches and will tell you straight if something doesn't make sense!) reinforcement I went to work.

The end result was a collection of the financial statements of a large sample of films over a fifteen-year period and spanning every genre and budget. Next we developed an exhaustive research protocol on multiple critical elements of each film in our dataset. We then hired several PhD's in finance and statistics to do what is called "Stepwise Regression". The product we produced was a very reliable model called the FBIndex™, (Yes I'm making a shameless plug for this amazing tool!) which stands for: Film Business Intelligence Index.

The FBIndex™ is designed to allow financiers and filmmakers the ability to quickly assess whether a project as submitted has a high or low probability to return an investor's money within a reasonable period of time. We define reasonable as 48 months. Think of it as the FICO™ score for the film finance business.

Once the 30+ elements of a film project is entered into the model it turns out a resulting score that is further classified into one of four levels of risk: Poor, Fair, Good or Excellent.

Table 5

Reducing the Risk in Film Finance

FBIndex™ Risk Rating System	
⧗ Excellent	750-850
⧗ Good	660-749
⧗ Fair	620-659
⧗ Poor	350-619

The FBIndex™ is the first commercially available benchmark designed to distinguish projects that have a high probability of success from those whose characteristics suggest a high probability of failure. Think of it as the credit score for the film finance industry.

We use a powerful and tested proprietary statistical algorithm that measures and evaluates a broad array of critical elements. The FBIndex™ further breaks down the financial risk into four distinct categories. The value proposition built into the design of the FBIndex™ is its enormous flexibility. For example, if a project does not initially score well, you have the opportunity to change some of the elements to produce a more acceptable profile; thereby creating a more viable project from a financial point of view.

Caveat: You must stick with the resultant changes during the film process in order to maintain the score. We believe that deals that score Good or Excellent are what we call investment grade. Deals that score fair or poor should be avoided or modified to achieve a higher score.

Poor: 350-619

A Poor risk profile suggest that the characteristics of this film project as currently constructed has a high probability of failing to return its budget back to investors within a reasonable period of time. We define a reasonable period of time as 48 months. An investor/ filmmaker should approach with caution before going forward with this project.

Fair: 620-659

A project that scores within the parameters of a Fair risk profile is one that has an even probability of returning investor funds within a reasonable period of time. This quality of project should be balanced with sound judgment and evaluation of other potential projects that have a lower risk profile.

Good 660-749

A risk profile of is one that possesses characterisitcs suggesting the prospects of failure have been reasonably reduced. This is the lowest score we would deem worthy of a green-light.

Excellent 750-850

These project characteristics are of the highest quality. A rating score of Excellent has all the key elements in combination that suggest the risk of failure have been substantially reduced. From a financial standpoint, this project is a go.

It is true, that the index may not capture unique projects that are statistical outliers that in the past have done equally well in release. Think of *The Blair Witch Project*. We never ran the model on that film but I'm sure it would have scored rather low (and by the way, at a $25K budget there's not much to lose).

Figure 9-1

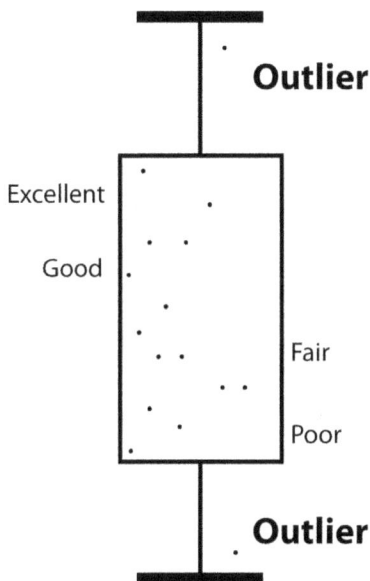

Our model does not try to predict the next homerun; it's goals are more modest than that. But what we are trying to do is protect an investor or filmmaker from doing something that has a high probability of failure. We call this In-The-Box Thinking. We have forward-tested our model on several hundred films and to date it has returned a 90% rate of accuracy.

To some skeptics, this may not be what they want to hear, and we understand that; however, just like credit scores it does not provide the whole story but a reasonable estimate of how a deal will behave and, more importantly, provides invaluable guidance in protecting investor's interest.

Some intuitivist (those who have relied on experience and luck) will still have a hard time accepting statistics or econometrics as a way to evaluate film projects; after all isn't this Art and not Science? Filmmaking may be Art, but film finance is a combo-platter; it takes both creativity and objectivity. But this is the wave of the future and it can't be stopped!

Statistical or probability analysis is used everyday from Google to ITunes, to eHarmony to Facebook and more. Almost every industry and government uses statistical modeling to determine outcomes. And contrary to some opinions, the film business is no exception. In his book "Super Crunchers", Ian Ayers says about statistical modeling:

> *Super Crunchers are not just invading and displacing traditional experts; they're changing our lives. They're not just changing the way that decisions are made; they're changing the decisions themselves... Super Crunchers and experts, of course, don't' always disagree. Number crunching sometimes confirms traditional wisdom. The world isn't so perverse that the traditional experts are wrong 100 percent of the time or were even no better than chance. Still number crunching is leading decision makers to make different and, by and large better choices.*

Smart money says don't fight it — embrace it! And you too will be ahead of the curve!

To be honest, the FBIndex™ is a powerful tool but it's just that: a tool! I'm not trying to convince you that you put all the values in the model and — voila! — you have an executive decision maker! Nothing substitutes good sense; however, an informed decision maker is better equipped to handle the complexities of film finance.

We believe that the FBIndex™ is exactly what investors and filmmakers alike have needed to provide a model that allows them to compare deals from an apple-to-apple standpoint without bias. But that's not all. We also believe that reliable Financial Ultimates are equally needed in order to really understand the upside and downside possibilities for each deal.

Film Business Intelligence is not the sole possession of the wise; it's within reach for all of us who want to utilize the best decision-making tools available.

Chapter 10

Bull**** Detector

Clues To Ensure Your Deal Is Real

How do you know when what you are hearing is shady?

In every business where opportunity to gain fame and fortune is significant, coupled with a low barrier of entry, you will find those who want to take advantage of others. Fortunately, they are in the minority. But nevertheless, there are a few clues that filmmakers and film financiers need to look out for.

Clue 1: Show Me The Money

Filmmakers need to watch out for deals that sound too good. Recently there have been a number of finance companies that have promised eighty percent (80%) of the financing if the filmmaker can put up or raise the remaining twenty percent (20%). These types of deals are fraught with problems.

First of all, they require that the 20% raised by the filmmaker is spent first; then the remaining 80% will kick in. What the filmmaker does not know is that, after they have spent their 20% and the financier has title to the project, suddenly there are problems getting to the remaining 80%. This is a scheme to get title rights without coming through with their portion of the financing.

Also, don't fall for the old 'let's put in escrow' scam. Usually it's an escrow account controlled by the scammer and buried in the escrow documents allows from them to siphon off fees and other expenses.

We all know that there are plenty of Russian Billionaires (for the record, I have no issues with Russian Billionaires) running around flush with oil money. That fact allows many opportunities for impersonation. I remember a deal that was brought to us for vetting. We were presented with bank statements that were in Rubles. There was no way to verify the bank or the money. So make sure that the money can be validated and converted into the currency of choice. But beware: bank statements, financial statements, and tax returns can be doctored.

I know I don't have to say this but I can't help it: watch out for those networking sites (I won't mention them here but you know the ones I'm talking about): there is a scam a day on them!

In my early days of banking when I was low man on the loan-officer totem pole, we used to get a Pink Alert Bulletin warning of Nigerian Fraud Teams (just like the Russians, I have no issue with the Nigerian people) working the area. Nothing has changed! Why? Because they work! The only thing that has changed is that their schemes have moved onto the Internet. The reason they work is because over time (at least 35 years of my experience) they have honed their ability to expertly appeal to human greed and/or compassion to the point of it being institutionalized.

Clue 2: Pay Me so I Can Pay You

Some finders (those who find money for projects) sometimes masquerade as financiers. Believe me, finders are very important to this business. But legitimate finders do not require that you pay an up front fee before service is rendered (unless they are also Packaging the deal). It's important to ask the right questions to find out whom you are working with. Also, keep in mind: finders are legally limited as to what they can or cannot do in terms of representation and negotiation.

If you don't know how to validate a potential investor, pay someone to do it for you. You need to know that they have the money in a liquid account which they control and that the money is clean as respects to any money laundering and Know Your Client (KYC) issues.

Clue 3: Verifiable Trust

As an investor, make sure your money is escrowed. Do not turnover any funds until you have validated a clear chain of title for the rights to the intellectual property.

This also goes for filmmakers. Filmmakers have a tendency to get excited when someone shows interest in their project. It is natural to have a heady feeling when you are only steps away from getting your deal done. Never let intimidation prevent you from asking them to validate their claims. If this scares them away: good for you!

Clue 4: Can You Walk Away?

I have often said that the best deals are struck at the point where both parties are willing to walk away. This means that you have gotten all the concessions you're going to get.

The reason it has to be a Win/ Win (See Getting to Fair in Chapter 5) situation for all is because people will steal what they think they have gotten cheated out of, whether it is time, money, equipment, or information. Don't fall into this trap!

Clue 5: What Does "In The Can Mean?"

Make sure that you the investor understand the film-making process as best you can. Not so much however that you try to control the filmmaker; this won't work and you may end up with a platypus of a film!

What is necessary is to understand what you are paying for. If you are financing the production budget, remember that there are post-production expenses that are critical, such as Negative Duplications (Prints) and Still Photographs for advertising (Ad's). Also, make sure that you have all the music clearances. All these items (and others) are needed so they can be turned over to the Distributor. If you have the distributor do all this for you, expect to pay an additional 30-40% markup on these cost.

When you have all the Deliverables (Including clear chain of title) then your film project is "In The Can"!

Chapter 11

Filming Is The Easy Part!

Every film is (or at least should be) a Special Purpose Entity (SPE). In Layman's terms, this means a separate legal and financial company bankruptcy remote from the principals.

There are many books and experts on how to form a SPE that meets the Securities and Exchange Commission (SEC) rules and regulations; therefore, we will not go into all the specifics of this area. These rules restrict from whom and how you can solicit money for your project. The recent passage of the Jumpstart Our Business Startups (JOBS) Act has modified some of the requirements (such as rule 506 regarding Crowd Solicitation) but you still need to do your homework (and contact a professional CPA or Securities Lawyer) so as to not run afoul of the SEC and the IRS.

Suffice it to say, form and structure of the SPE is critically important, and cannot and should not be over looked. Make sure you get competent legal and financial advice!

Some filmmakers (for good reason) are afraid to share their ideas out fear of theft. But unless you share it, that's all it will ever be: an idea that never got done. Make sure you have your intellectual property registered with The United States Copyright office (www.copyright.gov) and the WGA or Writers Guild (www.wga.org). This will add some protection to your Intellectual Property. You can also have people you pitch to sign a NDA (Non Disclosure Agreement) or a CA (Confidentiality Agreement). There are times when this is appropriate and other times when it's a little more difficult or delicate.

CHAPTER 12

Crowd Funding v. Professional Funding

"EXTRAORDINARY POPULAR DELUSIONS AND THE MADNESS OF CROWDS."

Charles Mackay 1841

The above quote was taken from Charles Mackay's book of the same name. Mr. Mackay's book was a humorous look at the history of investing Manias from the great Tulip Mania of the 15th Century to the Florida Land Mania of 19th Century. His point was to highlight how we as humans are poised to jump on one bandwagon after the next (think about Real Estate, Wall Street & Gold over the last decade) if it offers us an easy way to make money. This desire for easy money seems to be in our DNA!

If you are reading this book you probably know that wealth without work is rarely appreciated, respected, or preserved.

Money needs to be employed properly to function at its highest and best use. Some use the scientifically tested technique of throwing it at the wall of ideas and seeing if it sticks — receiving the requisite results. The fact is, not all great ideas get funded, and even if they do, don't always succeed!

This brings us to the modern iteration of Crowd Funding. I say modern because it has been around for a long time, as Mr. Mackay has attested to. All you have to do is think about the stock market — this is one of the oldest forms of crowd funding.

What the Internet has done is made crowd funding easier (that is, until or barring any additional regulation). The real question is: does easy access make it better?

In some ways absolutely yes! In some ways absolutley not!

I believe that crowd funding works best under two opposite conditions: (1) when there is zero expectation from the funder's standpoint or (2) when there is measureable accountability to fulfill the purpose intended.

If the funder has no expectation that the idea will work or get done, then it should be viewed as a gift (remember: IRS gifting rules apply) with no strings attached and no disappointment, even if it was received under false pretenses. This gift should be made with a view that just merely coming up with the idea deserves funding.

I'm sure not everyone agrees with this point of view, but I'm being blunt about this for a reason: there are many crowd funding ideas and pitches that will never see the light of day and the money will go straight to the campaigns originators pocket!

Additionally, this methodology can be wrought with fraud! Case in point: recently it was reported by CNN that there was a Kobe Beef Jerky Scam uncovered by a team working on a documentary about Kickstarter. The fraudulent Magus Fun group raised $120,000 from 3,252 donors and Kickstarter was just about to transfer the funds before they got word of the caper and pulled the plug!

But the thing here is that Kickstarter, the company, was not the one who caught the perpetrators! The real heroes (and just by coincidence) were the documentary staff! This is no knock on Kickstarter by any means; I truly admire them for their innovation! However, they have raised to-date over $571 Million dollars and, when you combine them with other crowd funding site such as Indigogo, the numbers reach perhaps into the billions; is it possible there have been other scams?

Now to the second point: if there was a way to hold campaigners accountable for the money they raise, it would serve as a first line of defense against scammers. The truth is, we will never be free of fraud and liberated from the imagination of scammers; however, that does not mean that filters can't be put in place to weed out as many as possible.

How does this work in film finance?

It is my contention that crowd funding is an excellent way to raise initial capital for a film project. By initial, I am referring to the Development Stage (See Chapter 1). Typically this is the exploratory stage where friends & family make up the bulk of donors. Ask anyone who has started a crowd funding campaign where most of their money came from: they will most likely say friends & family with a few well-wishers thrown in for good measure.

The reason I'm not so keen on the idea of funding a full budget (not small amounts under $50,000) is because there is no accountability.

As I said earlier, not all projects should get funded. This is because the rule of mutual exclusion applies. This rules mean that if project (a) gets funded it may exclude project (b) from getting funded (or at least delayed). Why? There is only so such much money available for film finance and not enough for all the conceivable projects to be funded!

Furthermore, not all projects are created and conceived equally. That is why our business needs to have filters imbedded in the process. Some of these filters, such as quality, and financial viability, can be (and for the most part are) detected during the vetting process. It's true: sometimes bad ideas and subpar execution slip through cracks, but this is no excuse to suspend checks and balances.

Why do we need these filters? Simply stated, they serve as a deterrent to funding unworthy projects as well as a means of protecting investor's money! When we talk about unworthy projects, we are not here merely discussing this from an artistic or preferential point of view (although this is hugely important). Our purpose is not to be film critics; we are financial critics (after all, this is a finance book).

Investors are precious to this business and we want our investors to re-up and stay in the film investment market! The best way to accomplish this all-important goal is to take good care of the investors we have and educate the ones we want to have. Nothing scares away investors more than losing money by taking risks they did not understand and working with people who prove to be unethical or incompetent!

Every great new idea comes with both blessings and curses. Most filmmakers feel that finding money for their project is uncharted territory as well as cumbersome, loathsome and a seemingly never-ending task.

For investors, finding an investment opportunity that provides a predictable and commensurate risk with an associated expected return is nirvana! I believe this tandem can be accomplished.

The takeaway here is that crowd funding and professional funding can and should co-exist.

Final Words

The Internet has made raising capital very straightforward; however, this does not mean in all cases it's better. What is needed most of all is discipline, accountability, and transparency.

It is our ardent hope that this book would be enlightenment to some, opportunity to others, and a pathway to all so that good deals will always find a way to secure funding.

If you pitch to me online, you can increase your opportunities for exposure, bring more investors to the table, help make the film finance industry more efficient and we can all move beyond the details and get some deals done!

ADDENDUM

FIGURE A-1

Ten-Year Ultimates

Project Name		Project 1	Project 2	Project 3	Project 4
REVENUES					
Theatrical					
	Domestic Rental	17,500	15,000	31,455	39,443
	Non-theatrical	1,400	800	1,100	3,021
	Foreign	4,240	7,500	300	17,351
Pay Television	Domestic	7,911	7,062	10,981	12,389
	Foreign	7,880	7,500	10,300	9,566
Domestic	Pay-Per-View	2,100	1,093	3,700	5,089
Home Video	Domestic	66,013	62,409	71,367	99,631
	Foreign	16,572	18,711	3,000	31,177
Network	Domestic	8,565	5,625	15,000	17,000
Basic Cable	Domestic				
Syndication	Domestic	250	250	250	250
Syndication	Foreign	15,155	13,700	16,000	25,000
Minimum Guarantees Domestic					
Minimum Guarantees Int'l					
TOTAL REVENUES		**147,596**	**139,650**	**163,503**	**260,893**
DIRECT COST					
	Negative Cost	31,357	19,500	14,359	20,706
	Capitalized Overhead	1,166	797	513	688
	Capitalized Interest	1,353	1,021	441	830
	Residuals	4,761	7,705	6,822	14,055
Theatrical	Domestic Prints	6,262	5,001	3,913	4,174
	Foreign Prints	2,172	2,765	527	2,971
Theatrical	Domestic Advertising	32,873	31,175	20,776	30,762
	Foreign Advertising	6,532	6,300	1,080	12,059
Television	Domestic	100	10	307	96
	Foreign	100	22	48	216
Home Video	Domestic (P&A)	30,888	29,488	23,842	38,835
	Foreign (P&A)	2,871	3,646	1,436	12,468
Domestic	Pay-Per-View				
TOTAL COST		120,435	107,430	74,244	137,860
CONTRIBUTION		27,161	32,220	89,259	123,033
Domestic Theatrical Dist. Fee 12%		2,100	1,800	3,775	4,733
International Dist. Fee 10%		2,729	2,870	2,660	5,242
Home Video Dist. Fee 125		14,411	20,061	74,260	101,102

75

Figure A-2

FBIndex™ (SAMPLE)

FBIndex™

Film Risk Rating System

(Sample)

Thank you for using the **FBIndex™ Risk Rating System** to evaluate your film project. As you know the **FBIndex™ Risk Rating System** is a powerful algorithm that compares proposed film projects to comparable historical data using over 30 data points.

Below you will find how your individual project ranks among similar projects within the criteria you submitted.

Project Name: Big Fun

Genre: Comedy

Budget: $7.5M

Rating: 760 out of a possible 850.

Rating Level: Excellent

FBIndex™ Risk Rating System		
✓	Excellent	750-850
☒	Good	660-749
☒	Fair	620-659
☒	Poor	350-619

Congratulations your project has achieved a rating of Excellent! Excellent is the highest category of the index!

The following are selected areas that your project stood out among its peer group.

Budget

Your budget of $7.5M is considered a powerful driver of success within the Comedy genre. Our research considers budgets at this level that are theatrically released as a strong indicator of generating revenues in excess of cost.

Above The Line Talent

You project was submitted with a director of known quality. Our research revealed that based on past performance the proposed director has added value to the projected revenues steams over cost.

Star Power

Our analysis considers not only named talent but also the combination of added value that talent has achieved historically as a percent of revenue. In this project its not one single name but the collaborative effect of the combined cast.

Location

You have picked a location with a very high tax incentive. This has added additional soft money that in turn has lowered your profitability threshold.

Genre

Your project is within the scope of a Comedy genre. Our research concluded that this genre has outperformed other genre of the same budget and your project outperforms its peer group due to the ensemble cast.

Overall

The above is a small sampling of the 30+ criteria of the **FBIndex™ Risk Rating System**. Please do not conclude that this list is meant to be exhaustive.

Changing of any element of the submitted data can and most likely will change the overall rating and can affect the prospects of the outcomes.

DISCLAIMER:

The **FBIndex™ Risk Rating System** is only one indicator of possible outcomes. It is not designed to replace a thorough and comprehensive project evaluation or common sense. Please be advised that there are other factors that the index cannot predict such as competition, execution of marketing plan, release date, and quality of performance.

APPENDIX

Terms And Definitions

PERSONAL

Biography (Bio's): Background information on the filmmaker such as the projects that they have worked on (filmography), career path, successful projects, etcetera.

Director: The person slated to direct this particular project. Some projects may not have a director attached before financing is procured. If so, this may also be a point of negotiation with the production team. A project does not need to have a well-known director in order to be successful; however, there is more risk associated with newer directors and will probably need additional oversight.

Producer: The principal Executive Producer (EP) in charge. This may be the person who has put the project together by selecting the project, director, talent and obtaining the financing. The EP is the main person responsible for the end product.

Writer: The person who wrote the screenplay and is the original copyright holder.

Film School: The film school the writer attended.

CREATIVE

Script/Synopsys/Treatment: The script is the completed screenplay that contains the sequence of scenes, acts and dialog.

Synopsys is an overview of the proposed project. A Synopsys can be a sentence, a paragraph or, at the max, two pages. It typically contains the WHO, WHAT, and HOW of the project. The "pitch" version of the synopsis starts out with: "This is about..." and goes on to tell about the three (3) acts of the script and concludes with the resolution.

A Treatment is more extensive than a synopsis. A Treatment sets out how you are going to treat the story from a dramatic or cinematic perspective. It is usually about 3 to 10 pages. It can be seen at as a selling-document that demonstrates the writer's full grasp of the story.

Talent Wish-list: This is a list of the proposed cast. It should have all the main characters listed with perhaps three optional choices in case the first choices are not available. Having headshots of the proposed character is a good idea.

Script Coverage: There are professional writers who will review a script for story structure, character development, commercial appeal, etc. They provide a written detailed analysis of the project/script and will give one of three ratings: PASS (rejection) CONSIDER (Good idea but needs work) or RECOMMEND (the highest level). I recommend that investors make this a requirement.

Sizzle Reel/Teaser/Trailer: If the film has already been made and you want to get the attention of a distributor or buyer, a Trailer or Sizzle Reel is an excellent idea. A Sizzle Reel is a 3 to 5 minute promotional video.

Most of us have seen a Trailer and I believe no definition is necessary. If the film is not made yet, a filmmaker may put together a Teaser (a series of short advertizing promos) to demonstrate what to expect from the full-length film.

Story Board: This tells the story from the visual perspective of the director. The director lays out the plot and main character in a visual form.

Log Line: Usually one sentence that tells what the story is about or what it's like. For example: this story is like James Bond meets Salt meets Al Qaeda.

Location: Where the principal photography is going to take place or the backdrop of the story. Location has a major impact on Tax Credits and therefore overall cost.

Genre: Any type of film other than a drama.

Language: What language will be spoken and if there will be subtitles.

Type of Release: Theatrical (At the Cinema) DVD, Webisode, Internet TV, Mobile, etc.

CIRCA: When the project takes place: Past, Present, Future or specific date.

FINANCIAL

Budget: Budgets come in four sections. the Top Sheet contains the cost of talent, including producers, writers, supporting-cast, rehearsals, travel & living expenses, etc. This section is called 'above the line cost'. Next, you have the production cost. Production cost includes in part: construction cost, art, camera, lighting, makeup, transportation, etc. Next you have post-production expenses such as editing, lab, music rights etc. Finally, you have other expenses such as insurance, publicity, etc.

Marketing Plan: This is the plan that sets out who you are going to market to and how you are going to do it. Some producers use focus groups to help steer their marketing campaign and other make good use of social media marketing strategies.

Business Plan: A Business Plan has all the components listed above; it includes the story, marketing plan, comparison and financial analysis and background of the principal team.

FBIndex™: The FBIndex™ (Film Business Intelligence Index) is a statistical model that compares a specific project to a dataset of similar projects to determine its risk level. Think of it as the FICO™ score for the film business. It is a quick way to determine a projects viability as presented. It also allows for changes in variables to obtain a higher risk-rating.

Financial Ultimates: Ultimates are the 10 year waterfall of income from sources such as: theatrical release, pay television, foreign sales, home entertainment, Internet, rental, etc.

Sales Agent: A person selected by the producer to represent the sale of the film. The sales agent can specialize in foreign sales or domestic distribution.

Pre Sales: A license or distribution agreement before the film is made. It may come in the form of an advance to help with production cost or it may be a minimum guarantee payable after the film is completed.

Sales Estimates: An estimate of how much a project may fetch in certain markets around the globe before the film is made. This estimate is usually provided by sales agents. Caution should be used when relying solely on sales estimates.

Minimum Guarantee (MG): MG's are the amount a distributor will to pay for the right to distribute a film. It may be in the form of an advance upon completion of the distribution agreement or it maybe a capped amount of the life of the agreement. MG's may also be performance based in that additional monies can be paid if certain conditions or thresholds are achieved.

Proof Of Funds (POF): A POF is a document that validates that a certain party has the available liquid cash in a financial institution. This can be in the form of Bank Statements, Verification of deposit (VOD), Brokerage Statement etc. You should follow up any written document with a call to that institution making sure that everything is in order as presented.

Type of Financing Required

Bank Loan: As the name implies, this is a loan from a bank. Typically, bank loans come in the form of Negative Pick Up's, Borrowing Base, or other collateral. Negative Pick Up's are made when a producer gets a guarantee from a distributor and the bank will advance a discounted percentage (e.g. 80%-85%) of the amount of the guarantee. Once the film is 'in the can', then the distributor pays the bank and obtains clear title of the film. A Borrowing Base loan is based on the revenues generated by the distribution of the film(s). This type of loan is used primarily when there is a slate of films to be released. The proceeds of this type of loan can be used for additional projects in development, corporate overhead, or acquisitions.

Bridge Loans: Bridge Loans are temporary loans for a short period of time until permanent financing is put in place. They can be used for Play or Pay situations or preproduction costs etc.

Development Funds: This type of funding is needed to help a project get off the ground. A producer may need to acquire rights to a book, a script or other intellectual property. It is also sometimes used to fund overhead expenses as a project is being put together.

Distribution: All projects need a form of distribution, either theatrical or otherwise. Often this is a financial arrangement that comes with an advance. Sometimes this can be in a non-financial form such as the so-called "Rent-A-System" platform. This is when a distributor (Studio) agrees (for a fee) to distribute a film but will not pay any advances or supply Prints & Ad's (P&A) funds. In this case, the producer will need to raise the necessary marketing funds independently. (See Minimum Guarantee for additional information)

Equity: Equity financing comes into play when a producer raises capital from investors looking for a share of the ownership rights and profits of the film. This form of financing is independent of distributors minimum guarantees. It is the most sought after type of financing and hence the hardest to obtain. Equity has the highest risk profile in the financing pyramid but many of the risks can be mitigated. Equity, if raised properly and managed well, yields the best rewards because it allows the producer to own a piece of the film in perpetuity.

GAP: GAP financing is the difference between the budget and the guaranteed minimum, or Negative Pickup (Negative means the film negative delivered to the distributor).

Matching Funds: Some investors will only provide capital after a certain portion of the budget (usually 50%) is already in place and will match the amount the first group puts up. This gives an investor comfort that others are willing to take the same risk as they are and have conducted their own independent due diligence.

Mezzanine: Means it is just above the equity financier and below the debt provider. It's like the floor just above floor #1 in the elevator. However, it has some interesting characteristics. It behaves like a loan and equity at the same time. Usually it's a debt that can be converted into equity if the project hits certain milestones or roadblocks.

Negative Pickup: It simply means the film negative (as in Cellulose Photography) being picked up (purchased the rights to distribute) by the distributor at an agreed upon price before the film is made. Before the film goes into production, a distributor may issue a guarantee to pay a fixed amount (budget) if the finished film contains all the agreed-upon elements.

P & A: Prints and Ad's monies are what is used for marketing purposes. It is the first money paid back from distribution. This is a separate form of financing from production and there are companies that only finance P&A because of its lower risk profile and faster turnover.

Product Placement: As part of their marketing plans, large companies want their product seen by as many people as possible. They are willing to pay an advance to some moviemakers to have their product displayed prominently in a film. These monies are paid in advance and are used as part of the financing structure. A filmmaker can have the script reviewed by a product placement agent to assess these opportunities.

Slate Financing: This type of financing is used when a producer or production company has multiple projects ready for filming. The bank or financier will use all the titles as collateral for the loan and will make advances based on an agreed-upon formula (See Bank Loans above).

Tax Credits/Rebates: Tax Incentives are offered by States (or Countries) to attract film production as a means to stimulate their economies and train their workforce. They usually come in two forms: Credits, which are deductions against expenses and are usually sold to qualifying local residents, and Tax Rebates. Rebates come directly from the governing agency and do not have to be sold to residents and are therefore preferable.

LEGAL

Copyright Certificate Number: When a writer finishes a project, they need to obtain copyright protection. The two most widely used registration systems are the US Copyright Office (www.copyright. gov) and the Writer Guild of America (www.wga.org). Once a work is uploaded to the respective service (for a nominal fee) the copyright holder is issued a certificate number.

Chain of Title: Title rights can be bought and sold. A producer may or may not have the rights to a certain work or project. They must be able to prove who the original copyright owner is and demonstrate how they have obtained the rights and prove they are free and clear to procede. It is extremely important that each previous owner, lien-holder or interested party has been identified and satisfied. Otherwise, moving ahead with a dream project will become a nightmare! A title search with the secretary of state and the US copyright office is a must!

Legal Entity (SPE): Since each film is viewed as a separate legal entity, it should be memorialized as such. Usually this is in the form of a corporate structure such as an LLC, S Corp, or C Corp with its own tax ID number that is bankruptcy remote from the personal financial affairs of the producer. This is an important step; otherwise any debts (personal or business) attributable to the producer can be comingled with the film.

www.ingramcontent.com/pod-product-compliance
Lightning Source LLC
Chambersburg PA
CBHW060630210326
41520CB00010B/1539